THE STEPS FORWARD

FINDING a PATH for a NEW MEAT and REGIONAL CHARCUTERIE

THE STEPS FORWARD

FINDING a PATH for a NEW MEAT and REGIONAL CHARCUTERIE

AVANT-PROPOS

Let us contemplate the big picture, at past habits and routines, to discern, if we can, a sense of how life really works, how it blooms and prospers or how it sickens and decay.

We hold deep in our core all the answers, the challenge is to bring them out.

Virus impact

In these troubled times, I ponder what is going on and why?
Here are some thoughts, some long views.

In the Anthropocene era, Society is supposed to be led by science. Man is expected to dominate nature and intelligently control the situation. We can assume that, but in fact, our leaders are tempting to manage the onslaught of the Covid19 virus, quite unprepared and more driven by the pursuit of political power than the benefit of society. Nature, so far, has the last word and kicks the human endeavor.

It is an old recurring pattern: Tsunamis, major earthquakes, tornadoes and hurricanes are in our present awareness. In past centuries, huge volcanic explosions (Mount Tambora in Indonesia in 1815, Krakatoa in 1883) have changed the World. Further back, asteroid impacts or huge lava outpouring have driven the evolution. Remember the Chicxulub event, which terminated the dinosaurs and made room for a tiny mammal some 60 Million years ago.

We are, as humanity, the latest deal in mammal evolution and, having been given consciousness, we have worked out an awareness of how nature works, and we were led to the pretense of bossing the World. We, self-centeredly, call this era the Anthropocene.

Too far in Tech, Soul lost

I wonder: is it instead, that nature in its infinite wisdom aims at fixing the erratic results of Anthropos hubris? Is Life, all encompassing, aiming at renewing its own harmony, which we have dangerously disturbed?

America has led humanity in the last two centuries into the discovery and mastery of matter and energy.
It has been done in an exploitative way by a society which has anchored progress in a system of individual liberty but also taking possession of land, animals and even for a time, other human beings, and allowing private property of things, ideas and money.
The civilization was set measuring progress in return on investment and magnifying the power of money.

The fast development of techniques and resources is still protected by the culture and the laws to support the individual or corporation to gain power, even when it derives in speculative egoistic absorbed exploitation of the system itself.
The whole system, ruled by money, is aimed at continuous growth, which is a physical impossibility in the current mode of values.

The Earth life is suffering in many forms caused by human abuses: The ominous one is the atmosphere warming, caused by the accumulation of CO_2 and other gaz. The ocean rise is a big menace. Less visible, beyond the attrition of wildlife and the disruption of the microbiome affected by pollution and abuse of the environment.

Humanity is causing the trouble. Society doesn't account for the potential damage. The illusion of self-interest feeds the economy entertaining the illusion of growth as progress.

The political blockage affecting this nation is caused by the defense and fear for oneself and the need to control power against others. It is getting worst and the big picture shows ominously that it is time for humanity to mature a little bit.

When I observe life as it works, I propose to include the whole of it, the whole universe, from the big band to the black hole. It is one life, from microbes, plants, animals, humanity, to the Earth, its realms, the sun and planets, our galaxy and further cosmic dimensions.
The human presence on this specialty planet Earth under a life-giving sun is quite a mystery in itself. But we know that there is much more to it than what we can measure or what we can organize as religion to tell us...we know it inside ourselves.

Let us look closer into this vast panorama.

Red and Blue

During the last election we saw the political drama, illustrated critically by those maps with the red country counties and the blue cities, it was in a context of competition, winners take all, conflicting.

In facts, the country feeds the city, the city serves the whole with education, medicine, law, government and finance. In the country there may be more landowners attached to preserving the lifestyle, the goodies and comfort and mostly the power. In the city more of the creative educated "elite", may become pretentious. Both are in the hands of an ominous machine: The Industrial Agricultura complex.

To serve the need for food, the system works depends totally on the power of monopolistic corporations and administration. It became dramatically apparent, in its social implication, when the Covid19 infection jeopardized the operation of key meat plants and dairies. The last rung on the social ladder became suddenly irreplaceable, jeopardizing the hamburger.

The industrializing of food production and the
correlating distribution of packaged food is lauded as a
great success of our civilization however, besides the
frailty revealed by the pandemic, there are other
consequences, which explain the pain and confusion of our
time.
Food can't be dissociated from health. The abundance is
contributing to the length of life, though it is very unevenly
available. The quality of industrially processed nutrition,
standardized as commodity and modified by additives to
insure longer shelf life, combined with stressful limitation
of life conditions plays a role in the prevalence of
degenerative diseases.
 As a symptom of the inadequate nutrition, this essential of
society function, the cost of health maintenance is nearly
double the cost of food.
At the root of the political warfare, between red and blue,
is the crystallization of the individual competition to take
as much as possible for oneself, may be seeing but not
acting to give to the whole as the way for well-being and
harmony. Winning has become more important than
creating. Taking more than giving.
 In the field the natural farmer invests many months of
caring and providing, growing the seed from the soil life,
nurturing the full vegetation cycle to briefly taking the
crop. Balancing the books is reflecting the real life only
when the value reflects the life and not the speculation.

Power of Money

At this point, a critical look at our society shows how much we have drifted from natural balance and vitality. We abuse the World Life with over exploitation and by disrupting the carbon cycle, we risk the harmony of the climate and of all the biome. We aggravate it by our physical and chemical pollutions.
The social contract, which underlies "the economy", is at the core of civilization. The three factors: capital, management and labor need to work in harmony. instead, they are warped fundamentally by selfish greed. Symbolically, money subdues managing, and both tend to drive labor into an exploited subservient role.
Money has captured nearly all the power to its selfish advantage. To put it more specifically, Wall Street, uses the Washington lobby, to its advantage, corrupting the national body politics.
The constitutional order is miss-guided by the lobbyist occult control of the senators and the congressmen. Hubris leads to abuse of power, negates the responsibility to the whole.

The Capital-management power of the large corporations, (visible as the cumulating of CEO and

President functions), using its domination of congress and government can influences, if not outright controls ultimately, the monetary system.
The USA have enjoyed the benefits and have the responsibility of managing the $ as the money of last resort for the World. This wider implication of the system has been menaced by the incoherence of Washington in the last four years,

We face also the inadequacy of the military power and our diplomacy to cope with societal World problems. The pandemic reveals the need for a World authority capable to lead. USA is overwhelmed with confusion. Nations are conflicting and cannot build harmony. Ethnic groups and faiths are competing for advantage.

Today in our confinement, with an awareness of the deficiencies of our current civilization, we envision how the growing crisis is suddenly undermining the system. Money and credit have chang thed nature. The Old is replaced by New dynamics. In this moving landscape, we have to find our way. Raising over the brouhaha, it is clear that at the source, the problems are caused by selfish interest of individuals using advancing technological resources, without consideration or respect for the life on Earth. The remedy becomes obvious: Intelligent management of resources in harmony with Life.

At this point, beyond the consequences of the pandemic, it is obvious that the enormity of the task of bringing back harmony with nature demands a new look. The problem is much bigger than fixing a vaccine and restarting the economy. The survival issue is to fix the civilization unbalance, which has been growing for half a century.
To remedy the distortion of politics caused by the abuse of economic power, and the concurrent social decay, a change of core values is necessary.
Symbolically we need a new key to open the door into a path to quality rather than quantity. It may be is as simple as a consciousness shift into the We instead of the Me, the self being consciously part the whole and serving life. It implies social responsibility and teamwork.
It is a fundamental move to create for the whole, instead of taking for oneself, individual or corporation.

Swinging Back

We have to move beyond the noise of the medias, which are also driven by corporate unbalance, to hear what is already active and see the examples of the New, we look into the new generations. The young intuit it, they see the wrong, they know their challenge. They still have to articulate, beyond the emotional, an intelligent way for the founding of an improved civilization, to regain harmony with nature.

Big changes are coming, commanded by nature. They will happen sooner than we expect; how and when will depend on the strength of the shift of value amongst us, the raise of new leadership. The need for more natural catastrophe to force it, like civil war, world wars or bloody revolutions as in the past is possible but not warranted, we can do better. If we change our values with a new unselfish awareness, taking the whole in consideration, if we focus on balance, in a natural way, we can overcome quickly.

The production capacity exists, actually it is an overproduction capacity supporting questionable industries transforming excess corn into sugar and ethanol.
The challenge is to rebalance the production for a healthier society; to adjust value, from exploitative quantity to intelligent quality.

The pandemic triggers a break of civilization, the field is opening for a new approach. As an encouraging example of the shift working already visible in the surge of real value. However, they are still mostly fed by feelings and intuitions. The formulation of a new social contract intelligently reflecting a new system of value is a tall order for tomorrow. Today, the critical spot of holistic food generation is already stirring.

To sustain life, the first essential is air, the second is water and the third is food. All the rest is contingent. All three condition our corporal being, our health and energy. Our human identity, our responsible, intelligent creativity can bloom in a healthy body from our spiritual essence.

It is time to bring the new awareness and a refreshed intelligence forward.

THE ART AND CHALLENGES OF CHARCUTERIE

A vision of the new paradigm for producing and elaborating meats in harmony with nature and for the benefit of all

Troubled times challenge routine and habits, feelings are affected and reveal a deep unease.
The basic needs and emotions put the value of systems established and supported by society in question.
Procurement and distribution of food is generating all kind of critiques and new considerations when its defects become obvious:

- The system provides quantity but neglect quality, with health consequences.
- Soil degradation caused and still causes large CO_2 emission.
- Chemical pollution and MGO affect Life.
- Degraded animals manipulated with hormones and antibiotics carry their tares to consumers.
- Feed lots are a violence to nature and pollute badly.
- The industrial-agriculture complex is too big, too powerful, self-serving and dominating, farmers, finances and politics, it may collude with big distribution.
- The logistics are too long, freshness is impossible. Packaging creates a huge volume of vaste.
- Very high volume of production batches raises the risk of spreading contaminants or virulent contamination.

- The size and nature of staffing in the slaughterhouses forms a critical bottleneck as seen caused by Covid19.

As it evolved, the system has been supported by regulations and subsidies. It is imbricated in the energy sector with the production of ethanol and in the heavy chemical industry with fertilizers, herbicides and insecticides as well as antibiotics for the animal production. Grains also are heavily involved in international trade and politics.

The nation took the bet, with agriculture, to go for volume by all means, making it a political purpose of cheap food, creating a monster hard to manage, because fundamentally, it produces too much for the American consumer to absorb the excess that the vastness of American fertile land allows. This is not going to change soon, but a lot can be improved for the benefit of the American people by planning and boosting an independent and natural way to develop the regional potentials. When big becomes a menace, it is time to see that small is beautiful when it is anchored in the true nature of the country life and will help to balance and remedy the system.

The industrialization of agriculture and the monopolization of the meat industry, coupled with the "big boxes" mass distribution, serves us with cheap commodity products of mediocre standards. We tend to relate to the products as food stuff, no longer the intimate relation to nature of our ancestors. We no longer experience quality in a sensory way. The notion of quality we may have owes more to advertising and PR. It relates more to imagery and concepts, hardly any more to the substance of life, to taste and well-being.

The system hides a big unaccounted cost in land and animal abuses. It is a karma we must endure together with the big pollutions it generates.

Microbiome

The natural fertility of the soil depends on its life. The microbiome recycles the fallen organic material. Insects, worms, microbes and fungi transform inert minerals, dead vegetal and dung into the nutrition of the roots to deliver the sap to the greens.
During un-interrupted millennia, the American soils had accumulated enormous quantity of organic carbon. With the advent of machines, fertilizer and later chemical herbicides and insecticides, the microbiome has been harmed and neglected. Progressively the soil carbon was

released in the atmosphere, amounting over more than a century to major part of doubling the amount of CO2 loading the atmosphere.
Today the goal of climate control is to stop the emissions within the near future, but not yet to reduce the existing overload carried forward.

Regenerative Agriculture

It is a growing movement born with the need to create an alternative to the industrial abuses, together with the organic movement, it is reconverting successfully degraded farms. It is taking the animals out of the feed-lots and barns and returning cattle, pork and poultry to a natural life by integrating them in crop rotations of pastures and culture of feed and grains. The re-created harmony balances and revives the microbiome, it reduces chemical usage and absorb again CO2 in the soil.
It is a re-invention of ancient traditions served by the best of agricultural sciences, but most importantly, it is the result of an all-encompassing view of life interactions on the farm, it shifts attention to quality from quantity. The pre-industrial traditions play an inspirational mode when we discover that methods and techniques which became obsolete or uneconomical were of great importance for life balance and quality.

The renewed form of production has a different economy. It requires higher skills and more hand on the jobs. It offers more and better products in a continuous local chain of processors and services aimed at enhancing quality and freshness.

New Man or Woman

It takes a new man or woman to fully apprehend the scope of the challenge and to habilitate the creation of a new function in society. One with and opening to the Whole to see the Good to be a Creator with a generosity of character. Able to take his/her responsibilities to contribute to society.
If the American dream has to remain true, the field needs to be straightened. All the obstacles accumulated by the distorting power of the giant corporations. The unfair regulations and the patterns of old habits have to be identified and overcome; this started already a generation ago.

Some of the branches of food productions have progressed or recovered more than the meat and charcuterie, because their structures have been less altered by the industrialization.

While the creators of wine, cheese, bread, beer and many other food specialties, have made spectacular progress, and awaken the consumer to a sense of goodness and harmony with nature, still, the independent meat world is comparatively struggling.

Animal on the Farm

Agriculture becomes regenerative when animal and pasture are integrated as a living part of the biome in its largest sense. Rotation of culture and pasture is essential. Cropping of green forage and returning nutrients to the microbiome is an essential cycle of life on Earth, the process which has accumulated carbon in the soils and sustained fertility, until the chemicals interrupted the natural cycle. Free to move and living on vegetation the animals pasturing absorb the living greens and restitute the elements for the soil ton thrive. They capture carbon and lives without hormones and antibiotics and contrary to their brethren in feedlot, force-fed corn and soy, there are no pollutions.

These animals will grow the natural way and mature in their own time. Beef, pork, lamb or poultry from these will have very different quality than the industrial bred, first, because they are not likely to be genetically altered,

second because their meat is not going to be just hard
overgrown proteins.
Healthy mature meat conveys the vitality of nature, it
carries the sense of sacrifice, the mystery of the life
renewal, the sense of place, it is part of a terroir. It can feed
body and soul. Establishing these essential values is a
challenge of great portend, it holds an equally rewarding
potential. It is a necessity to complete the efforts of the
Regenerative-Agriculture and pays respect to the new
quality animals produced.

The New meat and Charcuterie

Here we see the function for the specialized trade, the
double challenge of bringing forward the character of the
place and the identity of the animal, and of establishing
new products and services, creating new values. Free from
the constraints of the Industry, the regional meat and
charcuterie can maintain the traceability, It can avoid or at
least reduce the risk of external contamination. It can
responsibly deliver to consumers the freshest and
healthiest, most vital meats and products.

   A specific type of production can develop in harmony
with the natural conditions, the climate and local ways and
traditions of farmers and people, reflecting the Terroir, as

it is called in Europe. Already used with wines and some cheeses in this country. It is a new focus its purpose being to connect the experience of the product with the awareness of the place and the people of a territory, in other word to connect with a specific aspect and quality of life.

In essence, this renewed quality of work already exists, more farms are practicing the regenerative methods and few pioneering meat operations are renewing the trade, some produce charcuterie. Quite a few started in farms. There is a clear feeling in the intent and purpose of these new enterprises, and an understanding of true and right is not in question.

The movement is still coming from intuitions and emotions and is not yet supported by a full intelligent awareness at the public level.

  Two major change have to occur to structure the effort: The development of a system able to handle the animal processing is badly needed, which could elaborate higher added value products. College and universities have to enable the study of the craft an train professionals, as well as schools need to contribute to the formation of apprentices.

The Crafts

In America, the craft by necessity existed from the origin. Progress was imported by immigrants from Europe. German brought their "Wurst" in the 19th century, the Italians brought their "salumi" in the early 20th century, artisanal beginnings followed the capital trends into industrial corporations. At another level, mostly restaurant kitchen recently a few French brought "la charcuterie". The increase in travel and the important development of the restaurant business led many new chefs to train overseas and also bring back a lot of inspiration. In the meat product realm, the efforts remained individual, creating small niche business. Little was done to create regional specific meats and specialty products as it happened in the wine realm.

I lived the experience of these pioneer ventures, watching the one able to grow to significant size, successively being absorbed into the meat monopolies by acquisition and mergers the American way.

During the same time, beginning with the last century, while the concentration of power in the industries was building, the old independent sector was left to decay. Nothing was done to maintain the quality resources and craftmanship, all efforts went for industrial technology for productivity and low prices, whatever the consequences.

Over time the skilled European supply of manpower was replaced by cheap uneducated labor and machinery. USDA regulations and the raise of the supermarkets have progressively destroyed the local meat processing structures. Locker rooms, butcher shops and slaughterhouses have progressively disappeared. The skilled butcher craftsmen adjusted themselves to the staffing of supermarket meat departments and meat purveyor houses. The craft has been reduced to the cutting and trimming of boxed meats, handling of vacuum-packed meat products and making a few fresh sausages.

There are exceptions and bright examples of a renewal exist, still, they illustrate the difficulties confronting the re-building of a solid independent system. The Agri-industrial complex absorbs most of the attention of the administration. There are agencies within USDA assisting organic production and new developments at the farm level. Meat is a particular case, because of the effect of Meat Inspection, by its practice being a major obstacle on the possibility of the field to grow.

Inspection is divided into Federal "US Inspection" which allow trade everywhere. It is articulated for and dominated by the industry. The system is unadapted for the small regional emerging operation as is a limiting burden. At the State, County or City level inspection is usually part of restaurant inspection. It is a State prerogative and exist in different form and effectivity. Though these services fall under the direct supervision of the FDA, the meat aspect is strongly influenced by the USDA regulations, and a critical consequence for the local small operator is the restriction of sales to the shop, with no access to local restaurants, institutions or retailers, blocking the business development. It sounds un-American, but it is still the way it is. All started in the early past century when, the administration of Teddy Roosevelt, responding to the emotions raised by The Jungle, written by Upton Sinclair, launched the inspection legislation. It turned the world of meat into a special case.

It is one of the reasons, which explain the current shape and disfunctions of the system. Since the threshold to qualify for USDA inspection is, most of the time, prohibitive for the new butcher or charcutier, the only option is the local shop. Beginning there the charcutier can research and find quality suppliers, he can start production an develop his specialties. He can gain customers in house, but he can't grow and expand his business when the market open.

Maintaining his way, the industry is protected from concurrence.

 A new and very interesting thing is happening though. The changes brought by Covid19 have opened the internet sales for the individual shop, which can make good usage of USPS, UPS or other new channels; regulations meant to ensure safety will have to be adjusted, one can expect, in a profitable way for the development and accessibility of the new meat and charcuterie.

Planning

Thinking of a new system, planning a shorter and better flow of meat and products from the farm to the plate, gaining the support of the authorities, schools and administration to build a system fit for a whole region or State, with the expression of a specific terroir is a tall order. It has to be grounded on the integration of the whole of life from the dirt to the well-being and harmony of consumers. More regenerative farms, new smaller slaughter facilities, new plants and shops will bring back a population of trade people to the region, offering a significant renaissance to the local society and potentially revive and repopulate dying country small town. With time, it will raise the standards of the industry itself. it must, by nature, be developed as a network of regional projects. The respect of nature in the genesis of an improved system of production of foods leads to Terroir as the essence of a natural region. In America, except for wine or some cheese, it is hard to find specific meat products associated to a place, but regions with an identity exist. Some are to be found within a whole State, most formind distinct region within a bigger State.

Focusing on "Terroir" in all its implications for the foundation of a new, better short chain of meat production is central to the obvious necessity to re-connect the country and the city. It is a critical potential to improve many things for America at this time. Becoming fully aware and standing for the presence and harmonic necessity of natural Life.
It is high time for those concerned, for the agencies, the education institutions, the politics to think and frame how to structure and support such a valorizing project.

Pioneers

Many individually venture into charcuterie as a hobby, they may be carried by a deepening sense of ecology or independency. The movement is striking at the individual level in its many forms and varied level of experience, it is spreading everywhere.

Knowledge and recipes, which used to be ethnic lore, are now accessible by a literature of books and dedicated groups; in the internet experience is shared, advice is solicited, and counsel is available. The movement is very trending and expands internationally.

Businesses are popping up to serve the craft with accessories and equipment. Most find the meat directly at the source, field butchering is prevalent in the country. Today a lot happens in cellars, barns, garages or attics, it is supposed to stay strictly private, but sometimes families grow big, and friends can also become family. The major reason is that freedom is practically unlimited. The regulatory authorities tend to ignore the activity.
 Some of these individuals gain experience and confidence to risk opening shop.

 Then they discover the local inspection, they discover a biased field, where the system seems to ignore most of what they have learned and instead is preoccupied by a general fear of pathogens.
The paradigm shifts from the goal to care in making quality, into becoming a routine of procedures and avoiding trouble from the inspector. The regulations limit their freedom to build their dream. It is definitely a moment when envisioning the idea of the American dream becomes problematic. They discover the infamous HACCP procedure to analyze the production process, define the risk control points and what it means to verify them to the satisfaction of the inspector to finally authorize production and sale. It is cumbersome, little guidance is available and can be costly. It distracts from all the direct attention to

the life of the process to the abstraction of instruments and logbooks to register numbers related to a scientific theory.

  The further step, qualifying for USDA inspection and approval of all the HACCPs, it is a very big hurdle to surmount.
The regulation system is mature for a fundamental revision. Keeping the purpose of human health, it is necessary to reconsider the risk of virulent pathogens within the whole microbiome from the farm to the human and modernize the vision. It should consider also the incidence of chemicals pollution in sanitation. An efficient system would give more importance to support. Education and control laboratories should be made available.

  The few pioneers who are reaching mastery, have gained support of the farmers and consuming public. After they have gained the USDA approval, they are still handicapped to operate with scattered and incomplete resources between the farm and the charcuterie. It is a field still ominously dominated by the monopolies. Supply trade and facilities are lagging in a big way. It is a big obstacle, both for the farmer to access market and for the craftsman, to get slaughter and meat distribution.

  It is still the each for oneself rule in the independent meat world. There is hardly any government or institution guidance and support. USDA, it seems, should be a decisive factor having the resources and the funding if it were to see the light.

A new vibrant regional meat market

The vision of a strong independent regenerative and sustainable sector needs to cohere. It will have to encompass, beyond the local agricultural products, a regional flexible slaughter facility, the regional wholesale meat packing and different specialized processing facilities. The new sector of the economy will generate a vital class of highly skilled craftspeople and corresponding skilled distribution and specialized salespeople to serve a value market.
The public will gain in understanding the value, even the virtues of naturally produced meats. People will relate to quality differently. Visibility and viability of quality meats will change the whole balance with the industry for the better.

Rebuilding the skills and capacity within a realigned system to gain critical speed, and to facilitate the growth of a renewed food economy cannot be neglected, imperiously

a necessity for society to face and reacts to the consequences of the monopolistic agri-industry.
The completion of a necessary local infra structure is a fundamental move, for which the resources exist. America created colleges and land grant universities, we have the department of agriculture, with an enormous budget and human resources, which can make room for this. Such a re-alignment is in tune with the growing demand of the public. It will have positive effect on the industry. A new qualified manpower will be able to sustain quality. It will have a positive effect on general health. It will enlarge the market for quality meats and allow it to catch-up with cheese and wine and it certainly could potentiate the latent value of American terroirs. This would be a great gain for the whole American society.

The reaction to the excess has been building now for a long time. Ecology in the wide world and Natural became a concept opposed to chemical or industrial for consumer items and food, it led to the creation of the organic and regenerating agriculture movements.

Terroir

    While the industry is preoccupied by the standardization
of commodity, the organic and regenerative natural
movements are focused on an ensemble of distinctive
factors.
In the Old-World millennial tradition this natural concern
has found its expression as Terroir.
For the wine the notion of a terroir is simple: A specific
soil, within a homogenous environment, a typical grape
variety, a set degree of maturity, proper handling, pressing
and fermenting, finally bottling. It can be a single property
or a whole county.
It is accepted as an art for dealing with the grapes. What to
say when the complexity increases like for the animal
carcass?

    With meats, things get more complex, affected by many
more factors. The type and race of the animals, the type of
pasture and feed, the raising method, the slaughter process
and the break of the carcass into many pieces, the kind of
process and the mode of consumption. At this level the
Terroir will cover a region, it will have a common geology,
identic soils with a uniform microbiome, a consistent
climate, a uniformity of agriculture type and a set society
with defined values. There will be local animal breeds
raised uniformly. The region will be equipped with the
necessary slaughter, breaking and distributing facilities.
All of that to allow a group of skilled craftspeople to

organize into a form of legally recognized community to harmonize and codify products of high quality, which will be controlled but also protected under a brand as regional specialties.
 Terroir is how to understand the interplay of all the local factors: physical, mineral, climate, biome, plants, animals and people, expressed in specific products.

 The senses are essential for the refinement of the products.
Just think of the slow process of observing the feeding preferences of the animal, the comparative tasting of weeds and the milk, to progressively eliminate the bitter and acid weeds from pastures to get the sweet milk, required for a perfect Reblochon or Tomme de Savoie.
 The same process has to guide the perfecting of the fruits of the terroir vegetal or animal.

 While Europe has institutionalized the local grouping of producers who take responsibility for a local product to become protected and has structured the administration for control and protection. Products of protected origin or protected denomination are praised by consumers trusting rightfully their qualities.
 Americans tend to hang on those same meat-products from Europe, rightfully for their qualities, legally or contraband, whatever USDA does to block them.

We have not yet anything comparable in America, our patent protection system fits the need of centralized corporation, not the collective endeavor. Much has to be done here to adjust the system to a new environment. It will allow harmony in the life of a natural region or territory to translate into unique products with the right skills and utmost quality for the benefits of all.

Treasures are hidden in America's terroirs. The inspirational toil of the pioneers will lead to their revelation. The institutions and the administration will follow suit.

It is not a crazy dream, it is already happening in the milk realm, which happens to be regulated differently than the meat, artisans have re-created a genuine American treasure of local World class products, with a complete system of creameries, distributors, retailers staffed with professionals. The professions as a whole found a voice, The American Cheese Association is heard in the political sphere.

Instead, in a field where independent meat operators have been quasi extinguished, the movement is hardly perceptible, though active on farms reviving ancient breeds and methods of caring for animals and in the hands of many hidden pioneers.

In contrast to what is missing in the meat field in America, Europe relying on its millenary tradition has been preserving terroirs, products and value for quality. The variety of products is enormous. They are identified, recognized by Support organizations like Slow-Food and by consumers, their value is high, their ubiquitous presence is able to balance the forces driving the industrialization and raise quality overall.

The regulations are more pragmatic, less doctrinal, the European Union maintains schooling and apprentice paths for the professions. Regional groups of professionals are organized to take the responsibility of defining and controlling the standards and processes of the products, which once approved get legal protection; not only in their branding (marketing takes care of that in the USA), but in their substance and methodology. In Italy the "disciplinari" (professional regulations) for the protected meat products prescribe the area (terroir), type of animal, the feed, the weight range or age, the process and methodology and sets the standard.

What Society preserves there, beyond romance, has substance, beyond the traditional market, it is recognized by the taste buds of those who pay attention all over the World. It creates great value and sustains the economy of those regions.

"DISCIPLINARE"

Example of codification of a terroir product, elaborated by the producers consorts and protected by the Italian and EU regulators.

This document rules the production of the relatively simple salami.
"Salame di Felino".
It was established under the responsibility of *E.CE.PA,* as mentioned in Art. 7, it is the designation of the local "Consorzio".
In 10 pages it is quite compact, instead, the "Disciplinare" of the **Parma prosciutto** stretches on more than 50 pages. The codification of Felino gives a very good sense of the specific details and the implication of the team of many partners and authorities involved.

We can get an idea of what it would take, in this country, for a similar product to be defined, documented, arbitrated, integrated in the HACCP system and released for sale. Here, with this example we can touch what we have to build, we can size the scope of all the aspects affecting a single product. It implies a team-work along the supply chain and within the colleagues charcutiers.

Production specification of the Protected Geographical Indication "Felino Salami"

Art. 1 Title

The Protected Geographical Indication "FELINO SALAMI" is reserved for the charcuterie product that meets the conditions and requirements laid down by this production specification.

Art. 2 Product Description

When released for consumption, the "SALAME FELINO" PGI is cylindrical in shape, with one end larger than the other and an external surface of grayish-white color slightly powdery due to the surface development of a small amount of native mold.

The "FELINO SALAMI" PGI must have the following characteristics:

- Weight: between 200 grams and 4.5 kg;

- Dimensions: irregular cylindrical shape with a length of between 15 and 130 cm;

- Organoleptic characteristics:

Consistency: the product must be compact, of non-elastic consistency; Aroma: delicate; Taste: sweet and delicate; Color: ruby red, no spots

- Chemical and chemical-physical characteristics: total proteins min. 23% collagen/protein ratio max 0.10 water/protein ratio max 2.00 fat/protein ratio 1,5/. pH max > 5,3/
Total lactobacilli >100,000

<u>Art. 3 Production Area</u>

The production area of the "SALAME FELINO" PGI is identified in the administrative territory of the Province of Parma.

<u>Art. 4 Proof of origin</u>

Each stage of the production process is monitored by documenting inputs and outputs for each. In this way, and through the registration in special lists, managed by the the control structure of breeders, butchers, meat wholesalers, producers, seasoners (driers) and packers/portioners, as well as through the timely declaration to the control structure of the quantities produced, the traceability of the product is guaranteed. All persons, whether natural or legal, entered in the relevant lists, are subject to control by the control structure, in accordance with the provisions of the production specification and its control plan.

<u>*Art. 5 Method of Production*</u>

The "FELINO SALAMI" PGI is obtained from the pork below:

- Pure or derived animals of the traditional breeds of Large White and Landrace base are allowed, as improved by the Italian Genealogical Book.

- Animals derived from the Duroc breed are also allowed, as improved by the Italian Genealogical Book.

- Animals of other breeds, meths and hybrids shall also be permitted, provided that their carcasses fall within classes U R O as defined in the Community classification table for pig carcasses referred to in Annex V to Reg. (EC) 1234/2007 and subsequent amendments.

- In compliance with tradition, carriers of antithetical characteristics remain excluded, with particular reference to stress sensitivity (PSS), which can now be objectively detected also on "post mortem" animals and dried/aged products.

- Pure animals of the Landrace Belga, Hampshire, Pietrain, Duroc and Spotted Poland breeds are excluded.

- The genetic types used must ensure the achievement of high weights with good efficiencies and, in any case, an average weight per batch (live weight) of 160 kilograms plus or minus 10%.

- The minimum slaughter age is nine months.

- The use of boars and sows is excluded.

- Pigs must be slaughtered in excellent health and perfectly bled dry.

The cuts of meat used in the production of the "SALAME FELINO" PGI consist of selected muscle and fat fractions such as, for example, belly and/or shoulder. The meat used must not have undergone any freezing process.

Muscle and fat fractions are carefully mixed by removing larger connective parts and soft adipose tissue. The meat (muscle and adipose fraction) used for the "SALAME FELINO" PGI must be stored in a cold room with a temperature not lower than - 1 °C equipped in such a way as to allow a good dehydration of the muscle fractions.

Grinding of the paste should be carried out with meat grinder (stamps with holes of 6-8 mm).

The meat is then kneaded with salt as a percentage from 2.0 to 2.8, whole pepper and/or pieces in percentage from 0.03 to 0.06 and crushed garlic.

In addition:

- dry white wine, with a maximum dose of 400 cl/100 kg of meat in order to accentuate the fragrance and scent;

- sugar and/or dyxose and/or fructose: 0 – 0.3%;

- fermentation starters: in accordance with good practice, taking into account the specific characteristics of feline salami starters. Their function is to develop flavor and aroma through the lipolytical and proteolytic action with color stabilization and acidification control.

- sodium and/or potassium nitrate max 300 mg/kg, sodium and/or potassium nitrite max 150 mg/kg;

- ascorbic acid and its sodium salt max 1 g/kg.

The paste of all ingredients must be bagged in natural pig gut (cular or gentle or filzetta). The ligature is carried out with non-mesh twine, with a single rope in sparse steps and hung with it.

The drying of the "FELINO SALAMI" PGI is the period during which under controlled humidity and temperature conditions there is the most accentuated dehydration. The drying has a minimum duration of 4 days and a maximum of 6 and takes place in premises specifically intended for carrying out this phase of processing. Drying is carried out hot at a temperature between 13° and 24°C and must allow adequate dehydration of the surface fractions in the first days of treatment.

After the drying phase, the seasoning phase begins, which takes place in rooms specifically intended for this purpose other than those used for drying.

Aging means the rest of salami under climatic conditions which may lead, during a slow and gradual reduction of humidity, to the evolution of natural fermentation and enzymatic phenomena, such as to entail over time modifications that give the product typical organoleptic characteristics and such as to guarantee the preservation and wholesomeness under normal conditions of room temperature.

The aging/drying of the "SALAME FELINO" PGI must be carried out in rooms where sufficient air change is ensured at temperatures between 12° and 18°C and must last at least 25 days.

The operations of slicing and packaging under vacuum or in a protective atmosphere must take place under the supervision of the control structure referred to in art. 7 in accordance with the procedures laid down in the control plan. In fact, due to the delicacy of the product, due to the potentially stressful nature of the cutting and packaging phases, it is necessary that the time of permanence of the slice in contact with the air is as short as possible, in order to prevent phenomena of color browning.

Art. 6 History

The reputation of the "SALAME FELINO" PGI is demonstrated by the copious bibliography containing references and quotations to the product in the subject.

The first references to the product can already be found in some Latin authors of the first century BC. (Apicio De Re cocquinaria).

The Feline Salami was well known in the successive courts of the capital: from the Farnese, to the Bourbons, to the Duchess Marie Louisa.

The oldest depiction of the product seems to be represented in the interior decoration of the Baptistery of Parma (1196–1307), where, in the slab dedicated to the zodiac sign of the aquarium, appear, placed at the turn of a revolving support of a pot, on the hearth, two salami that in size and shape, still current, can be traced back to the "SALAME FELINO" PGI.

In 1766 a census of pigs indicates that the Marquisate of Felino was the liveliest square in the district for the pig market, and at the same time calmers are found referring to the feline territory that list the lean and fat salami. Since the beginning of the 1800s the chronicles of customs and culinary indicate the presence of a particular way of transformation from pork to salami in the territory of the village of Felino.

In 1905 the term "Salame Felino" appears in the Italian dictionary and in 1912 the production of salami in Felino is

*considered in the report of the Minister of Agriculture on the
economic performance of the year.*

*The competent local public institutions, since 1927
recognize the salami produced in the Province of Parma the
name of Salame Felino, which evidently already had to enjoy
particular reputation and reputation, therefore also of
recognizability, if the affirmation in the commercial use of
this denomination constituted, in the evaluation of the Office
and Provincial Council of The National Economy, a reason
for promoting the well-being of the province.*

*Even today the roots in the territory of the province of
Parma of the production of Felino Salami can be seen
through research and insights on the gastronomic culture of
Parma. In fact, there are numerous reviews that link Salame
Felino to the gastronomy of the province citing it as one of
the most appreciated sausages of Parma, whose goodness is
inevitably linked to its centuries-old tradition that has
developed and kept intact only in the valleys of the province
of Parma. To this are also added the numerous events and
events that continue to be organized both in Italy and
abroad by the local authorities and provincial institutions of
Parma in honor of Salame Felino with installations of
tasting stands and dissemination of information material on
the characteristics and historical production in the Parma
area of Salame Felino.*

The production territory of Salame Felino PGI identified in the entire province of Parma, is characterized by the presence of hilly and flat areas at the same time and the presence of lakes and salt mines. In the Parmesan hills, it has always been possible to meet the technology of the plain and the salt of Salsomaggiore. In fact, also due to the presence of these salt mines, since 1300 the salting of pork and the processing of pork has led to the production of products recognized both nationally and internationally.

Art. 7 Controls

The control of the conformity of the product with the specification shall be carried out by a control structure in accordance with Articles 10 and 11 of Regulation (EC) No 510/2006. This structure is E.CE.PA, Strada dell'Anselma, 5 - 29100 Piacenza- , tel: 0523 6096 62, fax 0523 644447.

Art. 8 Labelling

The "SALAME FELINO" PGI can be released for consumption: whole, with only the label or any seal; in a slice, vacuum or protective atmosphere; sliced, vacuum or in a protective atmosphere.

The name "SALAME FELINO", followed by the mention "Protected Geographical Indication" or the acronym "PGI" (translated into the language of the country in which the product is marketed) must be affixed to the label or any seal in clear and indelible characters, clearly distinguishable from any other writing that appears on the same, followed by the Community graphic symbol and the company mark. The addition of any additional qualification other than those provided for in this specification, including adjectives: type, taste, use, selected, chosen and similar, is prohibited.

Individual competition or team-work

The EU regulates the responsibility left to the regional producers to codify the product. The National, here Italy, verify the conformity. The system supports the tradition, the quality and value of great products.

Here we will have to reverse engineer the process. It means:

- Understanding all the Terroir factors.
- Assemble the players, farmers, transformers and producers.
- Defining the product.
- Codifiy the materials and the process.
- Mobilize the authorities to establish the regulations.
- Get politics and public interested.

Associates

I have preached often for the formation of an American Charcuterie Association, but no cohesion has appeared

amongst the operators, so far. At least not with the scope
addressed here.
What individual can't do, a group of interessees can
achieve.
The list can be long, the most important it to realize the
scope of what is a stake, develop a vision and a purpose,
make plans and move step after step into implementation.

There are many fields of action:

- Professional, education training.
- Technical, product development.
- Sourcing, farmers relation, slaughter, breaker
  facilitation.
- Politics, new terroir concept.
- USDA, regulations adjustments, funding support.
- Institutions, Colleges and Universities research.
- Schools, apprenticeships.
- Industry, relationship.
- Restaurants, Retail.
- Public

Each topic is a world in itself and the list can look
overwhelming; it is time to remember that the trees can

hide the forest and the key is to begin the action with an awareness of the whole and a vision of the scope.

The ultimate responsibility will be to generate a conscious economy sector, rooted in and expressing nature with all the possible human skills, to benefit the whole society and improve life. Symbolically a shift from "Me" to "We" at the core of responsible creative activity.

The Field

There is still a long way, for meats and charcuterie, to reach the place already gained today by wine, cheese, bread, beer, and other preserves in shops, kitchen and consumer awareness. Organic and regenerative farmers as well, have quite a momentum. The market response demonstrates a readiness, even an anxiety to get more done. The public is demanding now healthier product, but also ecological jobs and investments. New generations demonstrate a need for a different way to value the products and the activities of our civilization. We must welcome it, since they are the one, who will have to improve our performances.
We need to look at possible remedies to launch the economy of the 21st century freely, in a larger perspective,

to be able to discern beyond numbing habits, where the system hurts and where it begs for change.
The major pains and the rigidities in the current system are rooted in the enormous industrial complex, the pains are endured by the society at large and the system keeps people's bellies full, but with growing damage to health and environment. We identify the pains. Next is to give proof to the consumer to establish new values.
In analogy it has been as if in a game, smart but irresponsible kids were left to handle gadgets too sophisticated for their maturity.

We need to clarify and explain our goals.
A lot has to be done, we need more hands-on deck, we need to catch the attention of the powers, we need to build the support structures, we need more outlets. The field is open for us, yes, we can do it!

We have a unique opportunity to create an expanded space for the local product, and develop a new way, to activate a new function, a new relationship between all the players, like a teamwork in which every player does his responsible work in his own place with an awareness of the whole game. Every player transcends the "me" and works from the "we" function. At every step in the game this awareness and focus builds the qualities gathered in the final product.

This transition to a new way, allows us to use all the knowledge and means of the past in a larger and freer avenue, it is awakening the Age of Aquarius.

The action is already engaged with many "proto-charcutiers", individually or with family cultivating the craft. They initiate the movement from tradition and pick some vibes in the air or from the internet. they launch their venture, self-teaching from books or from meat and sausage groups on Facebook.

 The craft is one of the most difficult to master, being so complex. It can be scary, when apprehended from the regulatory side, where microbes are frightening. It is much easier when handled from the sensory finesse, where instinct support the learning experience and smell and taste are the judges.
For the new charcutier, the world of inspectors and regulations will interfere readily with the learning. Like all human endeavor it is built on an intent and uses more or less up-to-date science to establish rules. It has its own habits and routine. Often perceived by the inconveniences it is in an odd way contributing to the whole by its function. There too, widening the scope beyond the pathogens into the full health balance, will allow to transit from the conflicting to the constructive.

Quality

Quality implies safety, it requires a mastery of all aspects of the chain, from the farm to the consumer plate.
It is true technically and spiritually. It involves all the agents: breeder, farmer, butchers, charcutiers, retailers, chefs, the academics and regulatory. All taking responsibility to respect the harmony of life, in its largest sense. Quality, that way, is food for the soul, it is what is best for life. Freshness and vitality are essential aspect of quality.

Quality is first seen, touched, smelled and tasted; it takes educated senses and refined feelings to recognize it. Eventually it can be described and shared. It is a living experience to relate with many aspects of the food to gain independence of external input, like what the regulators struggle to codify, as qualificatives, seals of approval or the implications of the food pyramid.
The current culture trusts the images of brands imposed by PR and advertising and ignore the substance.
Assessing true quality and its value requires talent, acquired by experience.
Advertising can manipulate the consumers aggressively numbing their awareness. The media dominate markets. With food the focus is mostly on price and convenience. In

our future, the role of publicity will be replaced by the advice and service of knowledgeable professional staff, creating a link with the source and the value of the product.

The Craftspeople

The charcuterie project will raise a new class of players in our economy. They will raise the quality of the whole system and they will create more value for the regions. Their role is to deliver a level of product and service, which maximizes the natural resources of the region and delivers more well-being and satisfaction to the customers.
It brings a change in the economy of the society, spending more for a higher value of food and service and saving on the cost of health directly and indirectly and also on the cost of pollution.
This transformation can only occur progressively and require a serious effort to organize the education of a new class of craftspeople, from apprentices to masters.
The institutions exist and the budgets can be found as part of a plan supported by an active association as previously discussed.
Today, skilled jobs implying a vast field of action and offering carriers in a growing field are the exception. The industrial food system exploits de-skilled manpower.

Tomorrow a new paradigm will attract more of the young, born at the dawn of Aquarius with a larger vision, more of a collective responsibility and pride in producing good. There is a stupendous creative energy latent in it, for a new balance in society.

Microbiome and Immunity

In the same way we look at the succession of processes, starting with the soil, ending on a consumer fork, when widening our attention to the whole, we need to look at the microbiome.
It is a continuum serving the roots in the soil, all the way to our own digestion.
We need to be aware of the interrelation of this complex and invisible part of life to understand how it balances itself in natural ways.
It conditions the fertility of the farm, the growth and health of animals, it pervades the stages of the process with a very specific role in the fermenting phase. A very large part of the craftsperson skills is focused on managing the microbiome. The life in the microbiome is dynamic and implies balance. It tends, like all-natural life to harmonize within the whole; it is not good or bad in itself. The bad is a perception we get from the way science, through regulations, make us relate to the

pathogens. They can be virulent, and the authority impose the paradigm of absolute elimination, to protect the weakest exposed link. It imposes again a cost and pollution to the system, which doesn't stand a holistic evaluation.

Full awareness of the presence and role of the biome at each step of production, remains within the scope of the professional, avoiding the risks inherent to the industrial volume, the technologies and transports long distances and time of mass production and distribution. Freshness within the regional trade, will create better opportunity to handle the microbiome on a smaller scale more effectively.

Food safety

  When the passion develops and you plan to go into business, you will be stepping in regulatory territory: **HACCP is the rule.**   It is primarily a scientific way to organize and control a production process, and the way USDA-FSIS will keep an eye on your way of working.

  Let **Trevor Morones** of **Control Point** explain:

Food safety is an asset, not an expense. Unpleasantly bitter, most will share their feelings, facts, and experience of food safety in federal operations. USDA FSIS (United States Department of Agriculture Food Safety Inspection Service) are the major leagues for meat, poultry, processed eggs. It will be what you make it, just like with the recipes: quality in, quality out. It has to be a structured management system. Say what you do and Do what you say.

An acronym with history in the 60's for space program developed by NASA, U.S. Army Laboratories, and the Pillsbury Company. *Hazard Analysis Critical Control Point,* applied "farm to table" based on common sense application of science, and technology to plan control and document.

HACCP, a simple management system covering biological, chemical, or physical hazards. Naturally occurring in food, contributed by the environment, or generated by mistake in processing hazards are present. With hazards present we use the principles to focus on preventing the problems to foodborne illness or injury. The systematic approach to identify, evaluate, and control food safety hazards.

Where do I start? Let's assemble the team. Some of the operations are lean, one or two people wear most if not all of the hats. Consider the bigger picture you are aiming for and think about the other departments. Contributing team member from other areas of the business will help ensure the structure is in place as stated.

Education and training are critical for HACCP. Success in food safety is not from luck, success stems from trial by fire. Working with regulators is another world. Understand that they are people, ask questions, request references mentioned. Operations greatest assets are the team members, treat them like the leaders they are, they are trying to save you money.

Now the question, is this for retail or federal?
It is suggested to go federal for the benefit of having a greater reach and some who started retail express regret.

Guidelines

- Generate a list of Prerequisite programs, the foundation of HACCP.
- Education and Training: Effective training is critical for successful implementation.

Preliminary steps

- Assemble the team.

- Describe the food and its distribution.
- Describe intended use and consumers.
- Develop a flow diagram.
- Verify the flow diagram.

The team is internal and external. Consider some of the connections created through charcuterie as an outside support person. Advisors and professors are encouraged. Before global travel restrictions, remote document review, auditing, and verification is practiced. Traveling and coordinating projects for 10 team members, signatures have become time stamped emails printed and attached the documents.

What is the end product and how will it get to the end user? This is where we start address packaging and labeling. The number one recall in the united states is undeclared allergens. Simple dry milk powder, minimal in quantity, large enough in concern to generate a recall. The cost of non-compliance always supersedes the cost of wholesome transparent business.

Guidance: When documenting recipes add an extra note; "CONTAINS –X". The allergen(s) are X. Listing ingredients, per 21 CFR 101 Food Labeling, usual name in descending order of predominance by weight.

Now proceed to how describe the intended use and consumers. On the topic of charcuterie, does one plan cover all products? No. HACCP is specific to processes. Generating several products under one process is possible. Think salame; multiple diameters, various flora, some younger than others, all created using the same plan. This appears to be a Non-Intact, Not Heat Treated Shelf Stable Product and the consumers are the general public (exception of allergy suffers).

HACCP education and training remotely or onsite, always have sticky notes for the round table. Using sticky notes, place one step on one note and post it on the wall in the proper position. Verify the process matches the flow of production before proceeding to the sevenprinciples.
- Conduct a hazard analysis.
- Determine the critical control points (CCPs).
- Establish critical limits.
- Establish Monitoring Procedures.
- Establish corrective actions.
- Establish verification procedures.
- Establish record-keeping and documentation procedures.

Now you see the plan, you feel the excitement of sharing in the building of a new economy. You understand the way of nature, the way of the soul and the life of the extended teamwork. You understand the requirement of discipline.
You know that this work is good.

You need to master skills to perform.

THE SEVEN STEPS ON THE PATH TO THE MASTERY

It is a long way, from the farmer's fork, to the consumer fork.
In the habitual and normal awareness, the ready meal is all we see. Much more has to be understood to cope with the foundation of our subsistence.
The one, who aims to master the art of charcuterie, has to raise his attention to a much wider field.
The meat is a very precious but complex ingredient, very demanding for its transformation, more so, than vegetable, fruit, grain, oil, or milk.
At all stages, the processes are complex, the microbiome always present and the products remain always perishable in different ways.

The conscious and permanent awareness of the responsibility for quality, rather than mechanical execution of recipe is a fundamental condition for positive results.

STEP ONE, THE ROOTS

Soil and Microbiome

The soil holds a complex life. Roots feed the plant growth, but also nourish the active biome.
Out of the soil, with the energy of the sun, water and CO2 the vegetal grows the sugars, starches and proteins to feed the animal and they releases oxygen.
Plants are the dominant form of life on this planet. Still attached to the ground they move as they grow. They are sensitive to the seasons. They live to give life to others.
Great vitality in many forms results from the interplay of the dirt biome with the plants and animals. Pasture thrives from being regularly grazed and fertilized by the waste of the grazers.
The developed soil can then yield, alternatively a plentiful crop of grains.
With time, sun and rain develop from each geological structural environment successive stages of life in a specific harmony, forming unique terroirs. It befalls on man to cultivate these terroirs to support his own life in harmony with his surroundings.

Animals

Animal, (Animus, soul in Latin). This confers enough individuality and freedom to beasts with enough sensitivity to thrive independently. Some have yielded their autonomy for the domestication. Man has taken the responsibility to care for them and got the reward of their labor, milk, eggs, wool and flesh, delivering a richer food to support his active thinking and creating activity.

From the wild hog to the industrialized butcher hog, we find many different races. All have originated in a specific terroir.
The more rustic breeds are able to forage for themselves for most of their life, like the black "iberico" for example, herded in the Dehesa of southern Spain, where in the fall they can fatten on acorn. As another example, the large white, prized by the salumieri of Emilia Romagna feeds on grains and whey, growing to more than 400 Lb.
There is a great variety of traditional breed with many different characteristics and aptitude, just to mention a few: "Cinta-nera" of Tuscani, landrace from Danemark, American Duroc, Mule-foot, Wattle, Berkshire, and Mangalitza.
These old breeds, hold the capacity to revive their adaptation to places and conditions and yield unique

terroir products. They hold qualities lost in the industrial pig.
Every breeder claims to have the best. My old friend Paul Willis instead swears by the farmer's breed, based on the fact that crossing improves vitality.
The raising mode, the quality of forage and feed as well as the degree of maturity are more important than the genetics, when it comes to determine the quality of the meat.

The industry developed for economic reasons a functional and performing animal to maximize productivity with big frequent litters, best food conversion ratio and fast growth to a standard weight, fitting the best norms and efficiency of the packing plant.
The consequent immature and watery meat is marketed as "the other white meat".

To choose the best meat for a specific product, one has to understand what qualities are apt to the purpose of production. Or, in reverse, one has to understand based on availability, what process to use for the best result.
For most product, mature pork carcass of more than 200Lb and a firm 1½ in of back-fat with a darker, drier meat, is the ideal.
As a rule, for traditional products the best carcass presents a firm fat with a higher melting point. It will work out best

during the processing and will yield the best mouthfeel for the product.

The "Iberico" finished on acorn yields instead an oily fat, which is valorized differently in the quality characteristic of the "jamon de pata-negra", which is so prized in Spain. The Mangalitza has a similar aptitude to build a lot of soft fat fit for a corresponding type of products.

The ability to evaluate a set carcass or the meats from a packing house and to determine how to best enhance its quality is a form of mastery. To choose the option of product, ingredients and proper methodology is an art. This fundamental process is at the core of developing the specific products of a terroir.
The meats of a terroir will have a type and characteristics. To recognize these and define the ultimate product, the charcutier will have to build on the farmer's work.

STEP TWO, THE MEAT

Butchering

From field-butchering or from a slaughterhouse, the carcass has to be broken down, the primal cuts boned, sorted and trimmed to become the best possible ingredients for the recipes.
The industry has simplified the break to 5 parts: leg, loin, belly, Boston butt and picnic. It is done very fast by straight saw cuts. It does not respect the anatomy and the secondary work of boning and trimming is made more difficult. It reduces the yield and the value of the final parts.

Muscle Fat Skin

 Let us skip the organs at this point.
 When we trim, it becomes obvious that the red muscle is actually wrapped in sinewy membranes, which connect and merge in heavy sinews attaching the bones.
There are well defined muscles with a sinew at each end connecting two bones, others bind several bones or attach on one side to a membrane wrapping other muscles and to a bone.
The wrapping membranes separating single, or group of muscles accumulate soft fat tissues, to cushions the contracting muscles.

The red meat is made of two proteins: actinin and myosin.
The membranes are made of another two proteins:
collagen and elastin.
It is very important to understand that the red muscle
proteins will generate the binding and will coagulate with
heat or acidification and instead, that the white collagen is
inert and will instead dissolve as gelatin in steam.
This is the first mystery to master!

The fat also presents different qualities. Very soft as the
leaf lard, it is meant to be rendered. The soft intra-
muscular fat is hardly better, it will be trimmed as needed
to avoid leading to smearing in the paste. It is more
abundant on the belly side, the most gathers around the
crotch, that part between the belly and the knuckle of the
leg can be saved as "la mouille" as the best fat to make the
emulsion of the liver mousse.
The more valuable fat constitutes the layer just
underneath the skin, its hardness depends on a matrix of
collagen tissue, containing the fat cells. The thickest and
best is covering the neck and shoulders. It is a fighting
shield inherited from the wild boar ancestors.
The skin is precious, it is made of the collagen protein, a
source of juiciness it can confer to cooked sausages, or
binding as a gel for pâté, aspic or broth. Contrarily to the
meat proteins, which coagulate with heat, the gelatin

dissolves and emulsifies with the muscle proteins, fat and water.
The second mystery revealed!

Here you may refer to the video published previously

The Art and Philosophy of producing Quality Pork products
https://www.amazon.com/s?k=video%2C+the+art+and+philosophy+of+producing+quality+pork+products&ref=nb_sb_noss

What is demonstrated in the video, is a method meant to respect the anatomy.
The purpose is to maximize the uniformity and size of the cuts, respect the intimate quality of the meat all the way to the end.
It is a skill to learn.
For the primal cuts, I use a knife with a straight short blade (6-8 in)to disarticulate and separate the leg from the body, then remove the whole shoulder and finally saw the ribs to separate the spine (loin and neck) from the belly. It can be fast and clean.
The further working will depend on the desired usage.
The straight knife is used for all the boning, a thinner and more flexible blade is used for peeling off membranes or sinews, the long wider knife for the large muscle cutting,

fat cutting and dressing a whole piece. It is also used to peel off the fat from the skin, which need to be as lean as possible for their further usage.

The shoulder meat is the most valuable for the making of salame. I learned from the pros in Italy how to, layer by layers remove the individual muscles, first cleaning them superficially of membranes and soft fat. Remove that way all the muscles until the surface of the blade bone is exposed.

The biggest and best muscles are the ones attached by heavy sinews to the elbow tip, the cushion and the three muscles, underneath the blade attached to the head of the humerus. The technique consists of reaching the head of the sinew attached to the elbow tip, then pull on the bone to get the sinew under tension, glide the blade on the surface of the sinew into the whole muscle to expose it, slide the blade underneath the head of the sinew, maintaining the tension and glide the blade to remove the sinew.

Next pull the blade delicately without cutting off the sinews attaching muscles to humerus underneath the articulation. Then loosen the humerus bone from the knee, biceps and cushion, hold it and pull to repeat the movement of the elbow/cushion and do the same successively as you clear the articulation for each central sinew of the three muscles. You can this way remove five major sinews.

Sorting

First job is to cut out and trim the whole muscles, which will be processed as such: ham, belly, loin, coppa, guanciale, adjusted to their specific purpose.

Second job is to gain and sort the meats. It begins with de-senewing the shoulder muscles.

To maximize the first choice of material fit for the finest salami and sausages and then proceeding from pure red muscle to rendering material.

- Pork I, at least 90% red muscle, 10% fat, preferably hard and only very thin sinews.
- Pork II, 90% lean muscle and sinews.
- 75% trim with maximum 25% of fat and membranes.
- 50/50 fatter trim.
- Hard fat may contain 10-15% of collagen.
- Soft fat.
- Skins, as well cleaned of the fat as possible.
- Lard for rendering.
- Head snout and ears, cheeks, tongue.
- Trotters and tail.
- Brain.
- Liver.
- Spleen, lungs, pancreas, salivary glands.
- Blood.

STEP THREE THE INGREDIENTS

At the beginning there was only salt and sun. Actually, salt sun and microbiome.

The salt modifies the proteins, the microbes produce enzymes to ferment and protect, sun and air absorb the released water.
Smoke might also be part of the play, per se or accessory to cooking.
Enough means in these to make any product!

We have become much more sophisticated today.

Salt
Sea salt, rock salt, refined or not, the choices are infinite; besides NaCl, oligo elements or other compounds can be present. The tastes vary and offers choices.
Salt binds and modifies the proteins. It is visible: color and texture are modified by salt. The red proteins of the muscle fibers, actinin and myosin become soluble and can form a glue when extracted from the fibers.
Salt screens the microbiome. It favors certain beneficial microbes, eliminate some and hampers other.

Salt in surface contact with the meat (dry salting) extracts water from the meat as a brine.

Salt combined with the acidification of the muscles, increased by the lactic fermentation, release the water initially bound to the proteins. (salami dripping during fermentation).

 Salt is commonly used at about 1% in the kitchen for cooking preparation

- Used at minimum1.5% in fresh or cooked charcuterie it is the trigger for the solubilizing of myosin, to build the emulsion of the paste.
- Used at min. 2,5% in salami and cured meats, to support fermentation and curing.
- Used at min. 3% to reach the proper concentration of 2-2.5% in the meat, in the process of equalizing curing of whole muscle, 3% takes in account the loss due to the extraction of the brine.

Wet curing in brine needs a balance in the concentration of salt in the brine, which can vary from 5% to10% or more (sea water is about 15%), with the other factors: volume of brine/ weight of meat/ time/temperature. It becomes an art in itself to do it right and consistently, because the brine accumulates extracts from the meat and a biome

develops in it, if you keep the brine for multiple usage.
Well mastered it can yield delicious flavors and aromas,
but it also can spoil.

  One can wonder why 2.5% to the fresh meat, which will
become close to 4% in the dry product, is still palatable?
The reason is that during the curing a large proportion of
the salt get chemically bound within the muscle proteins
and thus is no longer tasting as such.
The curing process is very apparent on the muscle, which
changes color and texture, indicating the completion of
curing. On ground muscle this curing effect is immediate
and provide the solubility of the myosin and actinin. This
critical change, activated by mixing, is the indispensable
mean to create the binding of the paste.

Salting
  When the proper mixture is ready according to the recipe,
often salt only, the salt has to be administered to the meat.
  The simplest is the salt box for small projects or the
heaping of salt over the yearly load of legs for the jamon.
These methods date from a time where the production was
coping with less hygiene and was primarily to boost the
shelf life of the cured meat. Consistent results depend on
the total control of: type of salt, temperature, ventilation,
RH, quality of the meat and time.

Manual handling has evolved into an Italian technology, using massaging and brushing machines to make 2 or 3 applications of a very coarse sea salt, the melting and absorbing is controlled by the set humidity and temperature of the salting room.

The easy way to control the saltiness is to use the equalizing process, by confining in a vacuum bag or in a container the salt and meat; the quantity of salt takes in account the desired level to be absorbed in the meat, usually 2.5% (same as for salami) and the portion of salt which will be lost with the purging brine, usually ½ -1%. One single application is fine, when using a bag. The time in fridge computed at 1-2 days/Lb. After the computed time the purge can be dumped, and the meat kept refrigerated for an equal time to allow for the osmotic equalization.

  After equalization the meat, which may have developed some sliming or surface molds can be washed and is ready for drying or smoking.

When handling multiple pieces in a container, it is best to split the weighted salt and apply for instance the half initially and the apply the rest at each turning over, two or three time during the salting (bottom pieces to the top and reverse).

It is possible to accelerate the process by tumbling meats like coppa or ham, to apply the salt and again before equalizing.

Other salts and ingredients

Nitrate

At the end of the middle age, the invention of the gun powder, made of charcoal, sulfur and saltpeter (KNO_3), introduced nitrate as a preservative. It is used at 0.03% max.
It is a low toxic, present in all green vegetables (fertilizer). It re-inforce the curing with two main effects, filtering off some bad germs, in particular the botulus and, as it is reduced progressively by the lactic ferments to KNO_2 and finally K and NO, it modifies the meat pigment and create a strong permanent red color (It resists cooking).
The presence of an active microbiome is necessary and is the source of more complex flavors, but it involves time and temperature control, required for the full curing to occur. Nitrate also affects biome and time for the enzymatic work of flavor development.
Saltpeter is used traditionally adding a special bite to the French "saucissons sec".

Nitrite

$NaNO_2$ is found in the "pink salt", 94% salt and 6% nitrite, to be used at 0.25% as part of the salt cure. So little is because it is highly toxic.

It plays the role of the nitrate faster and without the help of the microbiome.

 The introduction of its usage on injected bacon had a huge impact on the industry, reducing curing time by 70%. It was initially overused and poisoned consumers in the 1950s. It induced a fear of nitrate and nitrite which still resonates in the public.

Sugars
  Sugars are the small chain carbs, the sweeteners and are easy to digest, also by microbes. They are added into salami paste to support the fermentation, because of the requirement of the rule to achieve max. PH 5.2 within 72H. It was different before the industrial revolution.
In the tradition, a rested pig, properly slaughtered meat, still contains enough glycogen (muscle sugar) to feed the lactic ferments to get a PH drop sufficient for the hygiene of the process at PH 5.4-6 for best taste. What it implies, which the above rule ignores, is that drying has to begin much faster than the 72H limit, in fact immediately when the fermenting temperature is reached in the core. Drying may in fact be more important than PH drop for the preservation.

Longer carbs, like malto-dextrin or starch are used as extenders or binders, charcutiers can use them is some pâté recipes.

Water

  Removing the water initially bound in the proteins is enough to preserve some products like pemmican, biltong or the Inuit salmon.
Salt and water removal are the essence of the prosciutto process.
Salt, cure, fermentation and water removal are the essence of salame making.

  Water is added as ice to the cutter processing to form the finest emulsions of the Wurst.

Milk, NFDM

  Fresh milk is used in the Swiss "Kalbs Bratwurst" to wonderful result.
It is also part of the boudin noir recipe.

  The non-fat dry milk NFDM is a plain and honest band-aid for the charcutier. It is a natural binder. Lactose and lacto-protein can fix the binding of any paste from breakfast sausage to pâté de campagne, including salami.

Casings

 The purist will still clean and use the ones provided by the slaughtered animal itself.
We are dependent today to the trade for processed casings of lamb, pork or beef.
The industry provides many alternatives as cellulose based fibrous or collagen types.
I must mention also all the films for wrapping and pouches for vacuum.

Starters

 Instead of a natural selection of ferments and yeast from the natural biome, science provide selected types, often in mixtures meant to achieve determined results.
I opt for the development of a natural flora, adapted to each terroir.

Spices

 The good meat, handled and processed with care, naturally develop attractive color, aroma and flavor. No spices for the prosciuttos.
Spices affect the biome as bacteriostatic.
Tradition teaches that the basic: garlic, black pepper, capsicum add enough to the richness of aged specialties.

Ground and emulsified sausages, pâtés and galantines
require more spicing.
The immense variety of spices invite creativity, it is like
using color by the painter.

Spices can be abused to cover mediocrity.

STEP FOUR, BINDING AND EMULSION

Binding

I can affirm that there is no charcuterie without binding. The natural agent is the salt acting on the actinin and myosin of the muscle at a threshold of 1.5%, it doesn't change the chemistry, but the physics of the protein, which become soluble; they somehow, become similar to the egg white. They act like a glue able to bind to other proteins, collagen, water and fat.

That is our golden fleece.

All goes to ruin, when the oil from the smearing fat tissue reverses the emulsion. Good for mayonnaise, but the bane of the charcutier.

The Ph plays a role, The highest Ph in the meat the stronger the binding. That is why warm boned meat, which still retains a Ph close to 7 is immediately salted and then refrigerated to use later in sausage making. Industrial commodity meats at a low Ph 5+, are processed with an addition of polyphosphate to raise the Ph for the emulsion.

To activate the process of extracting and solubilizing, some physical activity by mixing is required, first to help the salt to spread and activate the myosin, then to extract the glue from the sarcoplasm of collagen, which contains the myosin and actinin fibers and finally to coat and bind all the particulates of the sausage or salami.

The glue does not bind to the fat as such, it will form an emulsion with the loose fat, but it will bind to the collagen matrix of the fat tissue.

This last key phase of the process can be helped by addition of liquid, in salami, usually in form of wine at 2-3%. in ground sausages at about 10% as water. In emulsified paste up to 30% as ice, depending on the desired juiciness.

The tackiness, which forms is the way to measure the effectivity of the binding is judged by feel, usually by the paste holding to the hand turned down, instead of falling.

The binding "glue" changes phase into a gel, which causes the cohesion of the sausage, when it coagulates from the heat at about 150º F or by acidification, when fermenting the salami.

Emulsion

In charcuterie the binding capacity of the salt-myosin is a fundamental aspect of the process.
In the perfect salame the particles of meat and fat cohere when the fermentation sets the paste. In many case ato bind the loose oils. In a sausage the emulsion is increased to hold some water and more fat. In a totally emulsified formula or a pâté the quality of the emulsion is critical. It must be a water-based emulsion able to bind oil to work. The set finished product will cohere and retain water and oil in the bind and achieve the perfect mouthfeel.
Loose oil is the bane: smearing. If left unchecked the slice of the finished product will crumble and the sausage purge and loose its fat when cooking.
Smearing is caused by excess loose oil, often due to the warming of the paste, preventing the binding.

It is why controlling the mixing temperature is so important.
Smearing can be reversed by the addition of emulsifying agent, like 1-3% of milk powder and more water.
But your honor as a master charcutier will be hurt!

  The final product can vary in texture from a hand cut salami without emulsion to a cutter made, perfectly smooth Lyoner without any particle. Most sausages based on grinding, will have some emulsion.
When the recipe calls for a matrix of emulsified paste and large particle of fat, like the mortadella, the "lardelli" are washed in warm water to eliminate the loose oil and expose the protein tissue to allow the binding with the emulsion.

  There are a few exceptions to confirm the rule: Nduja and Sobrasada are fermented high fat based semi-dry spreadable sausage based on a fat-based emulsion. The Tee Wurst in Germany or the Swiss "Mettwurst" are technically similar spreads, which are also smoked.

STEP FIVE, FIRE, STEAM AND SMOKE

Cased, tied or in the mold

  The content work is done. The paste has been stuffed, the casing linked or tied the pâtés are molded or nested in dough.

 All along the microbiome has been involved. All is part of a one life, visible only by its consequences, from the sea and the dirt to our guts. At this stage the charcutier takes control of the living process.
Heat will pasteurize the product. The critical temperature varies depending on the type and the processing; it is applied in many forms.
Fire, very high temperature applied to the surface, change the appearance, adds flavor and aroma. A real roast beef will take 4-500ºF for 15-20 min to brown and 275ºF long enough for the core to reach 125º F, which will equalize toward 135ºF and yield the perfect juicy pinkness. It is well, because the inner muscle is sterile and doesn't have to be pasteurized. The same principle of fire first and gentle slower heat to achieve the pasteurizing 150-160ºat

the core, will deliver the color and flavor without stressing the interior.

   This is where the quality of the binding will be appreciated, because it holds the heat and limits the purge of water and fat.
Steam is the most efficient way to transfer heat. It allows finer modulation and speed to precisely control the interior critical temperature, high enough to pasteurize while respecting the texture and juiciness.
Dry heat will generate steam from the product and dries it. Opening the vents in the oven releases the steam. It is done initially in the smoking process to achieve the right tackiness of the casing to absorb the smoke and get the desired color and aroma, the proper cooking temperature is then maintained by closing the vents to saturate the vapor and minimize the shrinkage, some ovens use live steam.
Here we find another trade off, managing the speed of heat transfer, is affecting quality.
The higher the temperature, the more flavor and color built, but also, the greater the shrinkage. So, determining temperature, speed of the air circulation when to apply steam or dry heat and time setting, is all the art.

When the proper temperature is reached in the product, it is often cold showered to stop the penetration of heat and to shrink the casing and create a blooming appearance.

The oven baking of mortadella in the very large casings is done in a similar pattern, the timing is function of the size, (6-8 H for 5-10 kg /piece, 2-3 days for up to 200kg giant mortadella). The first phase, vent open warms up the emulsion, the temperature raises slowly in the paste, leaving enough time for the completion of curing and for the flora to do a limited fermentation, the open-air circulation deliberately dries the mortadella, the baking is in a second phase completed to the core, with closed vents at a relatively low temperature. This way mortadella shrinks by about 10%, reducing the water activity and concentrating texture and flavor, it increases the shelf life into weeks.

STEP SIX, FERMENTING

Back to the biome.

We have to drive the life activity of the sausage inner biome, to achieve a specific result, the coagulation of the emulsion into gel by acidification. As a consequence, it releases part of the water bound to the proteins.

Inducing and managing this process is continued by drying and aging.

The starting condition is to have created in the casing a well bound ensemble of meat, fat, salt, a little sugar, some spices and a flora of microbes. Even when starters are used to inoculate the paste, there is always present a sampling of the biome coming from the origin of the meat and the environment of the processing place.

The medium of water saturated proteins and salt, with separate particle of fat is anaerobic, this eliminates most of the decay bacteria and give an advantage to the lactic germs.

The purpose is to create the ideal conditions, imaginatively "for the bugs to party, make babies and change the landscape" this view helps to understand how, the type of the paste, with small or large particles, with more or less of an emulsified fraction, sometimes with a heavy presence of spice like in chorizo and with the alcohol from the wine, makes for different "party" settings!

The temperature is important for the development of the desired bacterial activity. It is also a factor which will favorize certain types of ferments. As a rule, higher temperature boosts heavy lactic acid production, while lower temperature advantage mellow producers, who will have the leisure to also hydrolyze fats and proteins, generating flavors. That is a very important factor for the final taste of the salami.

The water activity is the other factor controlling the "party", the bugs activity slows if they get thirsty, stops when the available water runs out. In the beginning, the water bound to the proteins is released and available for the continuation of the microbe activity to support the acidification, even if the extraction starts early.
The ventilation over a source of heat and cold is the mean by which the Relative Humidity RH is controlled. The air-conditioning of the fermenting room allows for the control of the temperature and for the control of the relative humidity.
For the system to work perfectly, the paste within and the casing must remain permeable. In case of smearing, the free oil will interfere with the permeability.
The first job is to get the "party" to start by warming the core to18º C, with air circulating at 22-24ºC (here I will use C for convenience, since this technique is of European origin). It is warm enough to get the good guys working

and prevent the bad guys to intervene (botulus and staphilococus).
During this phase the control of the RH is off, vapor saturates and help the quick raise in temperature from the refrigerated paste. It takes 6-8 H. to achieve in professional chambers.
The second job starts when the core temperature is reached. The room starts controlling RH down to a low 50% and stops the ventilation when reached. The salami rests and transfers whatever water it can give out, until the air saturates again toward 95%. The ventilation restarts, to dry the environment and let the salami rest and transpire, without the flow of air over drying the casing.
 The phases will be initially short, with quick release of water, and will slow down over time. To accommodate the slowing, each day the settings are modified: temperature reduced by 2ºC and RH minimum raised initially by 10%, then 5%, then 3% to reach a low of about 70% in a week, and the RH maximum reduced to 85%, to insure the transfer to the aging room at 12-14ºC and RH 75-80%.
This proven technique offers a way to limit the PH drop too much and favor the flavor.
Fast initial drying helps control the development of the molding (the flower).
 It does not interfere with the Ph/time standard (72H/ Ph 5.2).

this process lasts about a week to set the salami and initiate the molding, on the third or fourth day by suspending the drying for a night or a whole day. By the completion the product will have shrunk by 12-15%.

The art of the charcutier is to orderly rule the party!

The dry-cured meats like coppa, pancetta and prosciutto, being integral muscles, do not carry an internal flora, and loose already a percentage of their water during the salting and resting, but they need to activate the enzymes and loose more water. They go through a warm phase similar to the fermentation described here. The Spanish style Jamon serrano and bresaola in the 30ºCs, the pancetta in the low 20ºCs. The same care is required to tune the ventilation and the RH to absorb the water as it is released.

"Salumi in sole e cantina"

The traditional simple way of using the available environment at the right season still works. Instead of measuring numbers the charcutier uses his sensitivity, a good precaution is to use thicker large intestine casing with bigger buffer capacity. The process was perceived in two phases: dripping and drying, taking the stuffed and bound salami from the shop outside in the morning sun or to hang over the kitchen stove in the steam from the cooking; another way was to hang on the rafters of a room and to bring burning charcoal in a pan on the floor to gently warm the room and when the salami changes color and becomes firm, sign of the coagulation of the paste, the window was open to change the air and begin the progressive drying. And then, when molded and dry hold it in a cellar to mature and keep for months.

STEP SEVEN, MATURING AND DRYING

Maturing is the time for the enzymes to work.
Drying is to ensure the stabilization of the product, the cessation of the internal microbial activity. It has to be a

gentle process to allow the external intervention of the biome.

Maturing also called aging applies to all the cured meats, salami and dry sausages.

 The purpose is to reduce the water activity to an ideal level for the type of product, to achieve stability and allow for the enzymes to do their work and develop the desired texture and aroma.

While this is happening, many products will benefit from the growth of molds and yeasts

  The modern equipment, the aging room, used for drying is functioning the same way as the dripping room. It is less powerful in relation to the volume of products. While dripping removes up to 5% of the water during a day, when the temperature is dropped to 10-14ºC, after the fermenting cycle or the heating of the prosciutto the rate of water evaporation goes down to 1-2%. The RH setting are closer, maximum around 82%, minimum around 75% and the difference will narrow when the product is finished.

  The self-made equipment of the private charcutier is usually an old fridge, modified with a new control unit to adjust the temperature and the humidity, but no longer with a maximum and minimum, but with a set point and tolerance margin. Set, for example, at 12ºC and 78% of RH. The heat is supplied by the environment and sometimes it is necessary to add a humidifier into the room.

The best traditional drying methods are associated with terroirs in the old world: The "Katen" (a thatched roof barn) in northern Germany, The "Trockener Raum" of the Grisons and Valais in Switzerland with their famous dried beef and hams. The typical plant in the Parma hills, build like a big apartment house across the wind coming down from the mountain, with the salting on the first floor, a terrace on the mountain side, to bring the prosciutto to the morning sunshine to dry and two or three floors above with windows on both sides, opened or closed to control the breeze flowing through to dry and age.

The drying in the past was meant to preserve meats for a very long time, and tended to be higher than today, the aging was incidental. May be not for the prosciutto which get a coating of "stucco" made of lard and rice flour, in a manner to cover the exposed face of the leg to stop the further drying, but to allow a much longer aging of at least a year and often several years, augmenting the time, for the enzymes to satisfy the gourmets. Smaller pieces like coppa and even salami can be likewise, cleaned of surface growth and vacuum packed to extend the maturing without loosening the best texture to over-drying.

Here is another way to cope with extreme drying, I have seen it done with years old Culatello, soak the meat for a while in wine before slicing, it works miracles. Just by pouring some wine over dry butts in a Ziplock and letting them sit for a week or so will do.

You climbed the seven steps. You master the fundamentals of a charcutier craftsman.
You can begin to experiment and learn from practice.
Many books and the internet are full of recipes.
You can learn more from other and get advice in groups on Facebook.
You see the whole landscape.
You see where a creative action is needed.
Your heart tells you that is your job!

Reviewed in Mammoth lakes, CA
May 13 2021